Published by Magna Books
Magna Road
Wigston
Leicester LE8 2ZH

Produced by
Twin Books
15 Sherwood Place
Greenwich, CT 06830
USA

Directed by HELENA Productions Ltd.
Illustrated by Van Gool-Lefevre-Loiseaux

ISBN 1 85422 050 0

Printed in Spain by
Printer industria gráfica sa. Barcelona
D. L. B.: 26782-1989

Little Red Riding Hood

MAGNA BOOKS

Twin Books

The mother carefully packed the pie into a basket for Grandmother, who lived in a cottage at the other side of the woods.

"Bring this to Grandmother. It will make her feel better," said Little Red Riding Hood's mother, handing her the basket. "And she will be happy to see you. Keep to the path, my dear, so you won't get lost. And don't talk to strangers. Tell Grandmother I'll visit her tomorrow."

Little Red Riding Hood was pleased to be entrusted with such an important task. She waved to her mother as she set off on her way. The sun shone brightly, and it seemed that even the flowers waved as they moved in the warm spring breeze. As she walked deeper into the forest, the trees' branches overhead blocked out much of the sunlight. "The path is like a delightful cave!" thought the girl, and she began to skip.

Because Little Red Riding Hood was so kind and gentle, the forest animals liked her. Before long the girl noticed that her animal friends were coming with her. The birds flitted from tree to bush, and the squirrels raced along the branches. Perhaps they thought she was too little to make such a long journey alone.

"It's a lovely day for a trip through the woods," said Little Red Riding Hood, and in a language that only the girl could understand, the animals agreed.

“What is that sound?” Little Red Riding Hood asked herself. She could hear heavy footsteps. Suddenly, a wolf appeared.

"Goodness! You startled me," said Little Red Riding Hood. She didn't know enough about wolves to be frightened of this one.

"Did I?" replied the wolf, thinking what a tasty treat the girl would make. "Well, I'm just out having my morning stroll."

The girl had forgotten her mother's warning not to speak to strangers. "I'm on my way to Grandmother's cottage at the other edge of the forest," she said. The wolf nodded, wondering how he could delay her and get to the cottage first. Then he could have both her and her grandmother for lunch!

Suddenly, the crafty wolf had an idea. "I think a bouquet of wildflowers would cheer the old lady," he said brightly.

"What a grand idea!" replied Little Red Riding Hood. "I will pick her some flowers right away. How happy she'll be!"

"I'll be on my way now," said the wolf. "I'm sure we'll meet again."

"I hope so!" said the girl.

The wolf sauntered into the woods, but as soon as he was out of sight...

...he dashed away, running as fast as he could toward Grandmother's cottage. "This is my lucky day," he thought. "Not one, but *two* meals for my hungry tummy." He knew just where the cottage was, so he wasted no time heading toward it, leaping over logs and dodging trees.

Little Red Riding Hood ran to find her animal friends. "Guess what?" she asked them. "I met the nicest fellow, and he suggested I bring Granny a bouquet. Now isn't that a fine idea?"

"I know where the prettiest flowers are!" exclaimed one of the squirrels, pointing into the woods.

Little Red Riding Hood had also forgotten her mother's warning not to stray off the path! She and the animals wandered in the woods until they came to a clearing.

Colorful wildflowers grew all about the sunny clearing. Little Red Riding Hood stooped to pick them, and in no time had gathered an armload. "What pretty flowers," she said to herself. Then she picked up her basket and made her way back to the path. "I'll have to thank Mr. Wolf for his advice."

The squirrels looked at each other. "Mr. Wolf?" said one of them with alarm. They scurried after the girl.

In the meantime, the wolf had arrived, panting from his long run, at Grandmother's cottage. He waited until he had caught his breath; then he knocked on the door.

"Who is it?" came Grandmother's voice.

"It's Little Red Riding Hood," answered the wolf, mimicking the girl's voice as best as he could.

"The door's unlocked. Come in, my dear," replied Grandmother.

The hungry wolf opened the door and glanced about the room. Then he bounded toward Grandmother's bed, and before she knew what was happening...

...he had gobbled her up in one bite. The squirrels and mice arrived on the windowsill just in time to see the wolf's misdeed. They looked at each other with alarm. "Little Red Riding Hood will be next on his menu!" exclaimed the squirrel.

"We must get help!" squeaked the mice. The animals raced off into the forest.

The wolf waddled about the cottage. He drew the curtains closed. Then he found one of Grandmother's nightgowns and nightcaps, and slipped these on. He pulled the cap over his big ears, then got into bed and pulled the covers up around his chin.

The wolf was almost asleep, for he was feeling full, when he heard a knock at the door. Doing his best to imitate Grandmother's voice, he called out, "Who is it?"

"It's Little Red Riding Hood," came the girl's voice.
"Come right in, dear," replied the wolf.
Little Red Riding Hood unlatched the door and stepped into the cottage. "My, it's dark in here, Granny," she said. "I've brought you a basket of food from Mother, and some flowers to make you feel better." She tried to sound cheery, but she felt very uneasy. She approached the bed. "Goodness, you don't look at all like yourself," said Little Red Riding Hood. "You must be very sick."

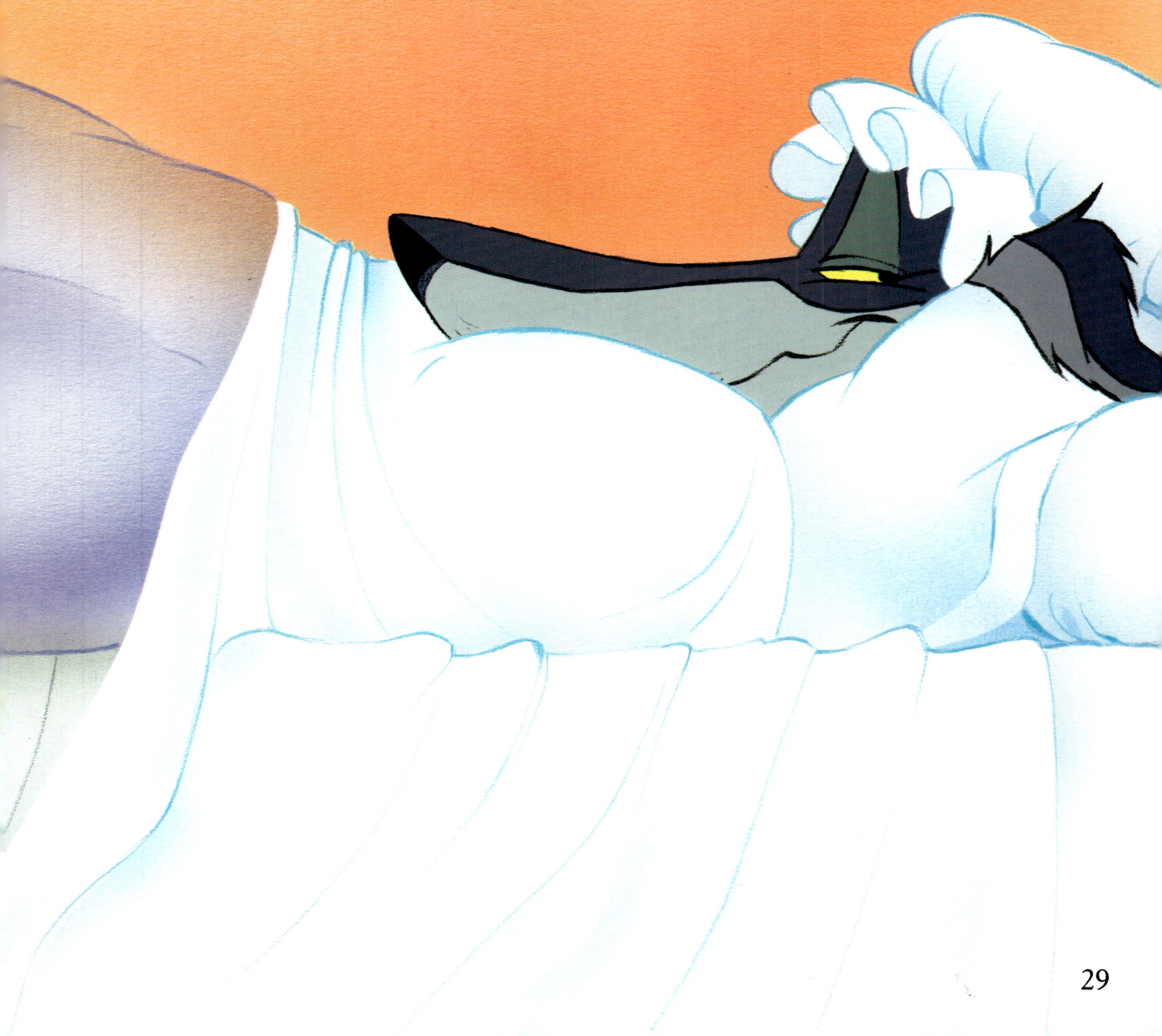

Just then the mice had found a family of Little Red Riding Hood's rabbit friends in the woods. "Come quick!" exclaimed the mouse. "The wolf has eaten Little Red Riding Hood's grandmother, and next he will eat her! Hurry! We must save her!"

The mice, squirrels and bunnies scurried and hopped as fast as they could toward Grandmother's cottage.

Back at the cottage, Little Red Riding Hood was peering intently at the figure in Grandmother's bed. "My, Grandmother," she said with alarm, "what big eyes you have!"

"All the better to see you with, my dear," croaked the wolf. Just then his ears popped out from under the nightcap.

"Ah, Grandmother. But what big ears you have," said the girl.

"All the better to hear you with," replied the wolf.

"Grandmother! What big teeth you have," she said.

"All the better to eat you with!" cried the wolf, leaping out of bed.

The wolf swallowed Little Red Riding Hood in one gulp. Feeling very full indeed, he walked slowly out of the cottage into the barn. He was looking for a place to take a long nap, and the hay looked inviting. As he nosed about, he felt so pleased with himself that he made up a little song about what a clever wolf he was.

The wolf was so sleepy that he took no notice of the mice and squirrels, chattering in the barn loft. If he had understood what they were saying, he would have taken note of them, for they were busy planning his downfall.

"The spade is ready!" called one of the squirrels.

"The rope is ready!" called another.

"Patience!" said one of the mice. "Wait until he's in just the right spot."

The animals held their breath as the wolf ambled into range, and then...

...*Bonk*! The squirrels let go of the spade handle, and it landed squarely on the wolf's head.

"Bull's-eye!" shouted one of the squirrels. The wolf lay on the ground in a daze.

Quickly, a mouse tied the rope to the wolf's tail. Throwing the rope over a rafter and threading it through a pulley, the animals began hoisting the wolf into the air. It took the strength of every bunny, mouse and squirrel.

When the wolf was fully suspended in the air by his tail, Grandmother and Little Red Riding Hood tumbled out of his open mouth, and landed on the soft hay.

The animals cheered when they saw the two were unharmed, and a bunny explained how they had performed the rescue. Little Red Riding Hood was terribly shaken, but grateful to her animal friends.

"I shall never trust a wolf again," exclaimed the girl. "And when mother tells me to keep to the path, and not speak to strangers, I will do just that!"

Grandmother laughed despite herself, then invited everyone to have some pie. The wolf, in the meantime, had dragged himself up and was slinking into the forest.

The wolf was hungry again, but even worse, he was feeling quite sheepish. Wherever he wandered from that time on, the forest animals remembered his naughty exploit. "Foolish wolf! Foolish wolf!" the birds would call. Then they would titter as the wolf passed by, pretending not to notice. And as for Little Red Riding Hood, she listened more carefully to her mother after her narrow escape, and every morning she scattered bread crumbs and seeds for the animals who had saved her life.